GOD'S LIVING WORD

Relevant, Alive, and Active

MARGARET FEINBERG

THOMAS NELSON
Since 1798

NASHVILLE   DALLAS   MEXICO CITY   RIO DE JANEIRO

Published in Nashville, Tennessee, by Thomas Nelson. Thomas Nelson is a trademark of Thomas Nelson, Inc.

Thomas Nelson, Inc., titles may be purchased in bulk for educational, business, fund-raising, or sales promotional use. For information, please e-mail SpecialMarkets@ThomasNelson.com.

All Scripture quotations are taken from the New King James Version. © 1982 by Thomas Nelson, Inc. Used by permission. All rights reserved.

Page design: Crosslin Creative

978-1-4016-7627-8

Printed in China

13 14 15 16 17 RRD 5 4 3 2 1

Contents

Introduction

The World's Most Amazing Book

"The Bible—banned, burned, beloved. More widely read, more frequently attacked than any other book in history. Generations of intellectuals have attempted to discredit it; dictators of every age have outlawed it and executed those who read it. Yet soldiers carry it into battle believing it more powerful than their weapons. Fragments of it smuggled into solitary prison cells have transformed ruthless killers into gentle saints."

Chuck Colson,
author of *Loving God*[1]

We tend to have books we prefer to read—whether snuggling down with a great biography, savoring a collection of poetry, or enjoying a mind-bending mystery novel. But have you ever considered that *what* we read affects *how* we read?

A good whodunit may make us flip the pages faster with every cliffhanger moment, while reading a rich, layered poem may slow our pace, inviting us to reread and reflect with each passing line. If we're sitting down to a short, light summer fiction read, we might expect to be carried away in the story—even choosing to read it in an afternoon or over a couple of days.

But if we're about to crack open a 700-plus-page biography, we can expect the book to be neither short nor light. We're committing to dive deep into a person's life and topic, pay attention to details, and learn with each passing page. *What* we read affects *how* we read.

In the same way, understanding the different genres or writing styles of the Bible prepares us to receive more out of the Scriptures every time we read from them. The Bible is literature. When we know something about the background, purpose, and writing style, we can learn to appreciate God's message all the more! Books of the Bible that may have appeared hard to read or disconnected from our modern world suddenly come alive in a new light. Along the way, we begin to lay hold of depth and delight in God's Living Word—not just as ancient writings, but as a book that's more relevant, alive, and active in our daily lives than we ever imagined.

In this study, we're going to look at some of the genres found throughout the Bible. We're exploring only a sampling of the many different types of writing found throughout the Scripture. I'm hopeful what you'll discover will whet your appetite to dive deeper into the world's most amazing book and learn to savor God's Living Word like never before.

My prayer is that through this study the Scripture will come alive in your heart in such a way you can't help but become just a little bit more like Jesus.

Blessings,
Margaret Feinberg

Sampling the Old Testament Genres

For some people, the Old Testament, also known as the Hebrew Scriptures, can be intimating and overwhelming. Not only is the Old Testament a thick read, but it's loaded with all kinds of historical details, records of the Jewish law, and miraculous accounts of God saving and redeeming His people. Understanding a few of the genres tucked into the Old Testament can help bring to life these important scriptures in your heart.

> "If you look at a window, you see flyspecks, dust, the crack where Junior's Frisbee hit it. If you look through a window, you see the world beyond. Something like this is the difference between those who see the Bible as a Holy Bore and those who see it as the Word of God, which speaks out of the depths of an almost unimaginable past in the depths of ourselves."

Frederick Buechner,
pastor and author

The Bible

A Book Like No Other

Andrew Frazer, a godly Irishman, traveled to California to recover from tuberculosis. The disease had taken a heavy toll on his lungs, leaving him barely able to speak. But while visiting a popular Bible teacher, H. A. Ironside, Frazer managed to open up a well-worn Bible and read the Scriptures in ways Ironside had never heard before.

Listening to the sweet words, Ironside brushed tears from his cheeks. He asked Frazer where he had learned his rich insights into Scripture. What books did he need to buy? What professor or seminary had given him such rich treasures?

"My dear young man," Frazer answered. "I learned these things on my knees on the mud floor of a little sod cottage in the north of Ireland. There with my Bible open before me, I used to kneel for hours at a time, and ask the Spirit of God to reveal Christ to my soul and open the Word to my heart. He taught me more on my knees on that mud floor than I ever could have learned in all the seminaries or colleges in the world."[2]

This story is a powerful reminder that the Bible is a book like no other. While we can learn much through seminaries and scholarly commentaries, God wants to reveal Himself to us through Scripture as we read and study right in our own homes. Unlike other books you read, the Bible doesn't only offer wisdom for everyday life or practical advice for sticky situations. Through the Holy Spirit, the Bible contains the power to transform you from the inside out as you read, study, and obey.

God has breathed on, in, and through the Bible.

Second Timothy 3:16 says, "All Scripture *is* given by inspiration of God, and *is* profitable for doctrine, for reproof, for correction, for instruction in righteousness." The word *inspiration* is translated from the Greek word *theopneustos* and literally means "God-breathed."

Think about this for a moment: God has breathed on, in, and through the Bible.

While a number of writers contributed to the Bible, often adding their own personalites and styles, the real author of the Bible is God.

The Bible isn't a compilation of good ideas or religious ingenuity; its origin is rooted in God. This is His book and His story. God uses the Bible to reveal Himself to us, even today.

Through the Bible, we discover God is good, just, kind, loving, merciful, eternal, and gracious. We learn God is sovereign and true. We catch glimpses of God's power as the One who created and holds all things together. In the Bible, we find not only that God goes to incredible lengths to invite people into a relationship with Himself, but also the consequences of those who choose to reject the loving invitation of God. The Bible also records the many promises and plans of God.

If we want to know God and recognize His voice and presence in our lives, the Bible is the foundation and the filter for this journey. Scripture helps us to grow into mature Jesus followers, learn from our mistakes, and become all God has called and created us to be.

✛ Three Things to Remember

- The Bible is the primary way God communicates and reveals Himself to His people.

- As we spend time reading, studying, and obeying the Scripture, we can't help but be transformed into the likeness of Christ and grow in spiritual maturity.

- If you're struggling to read your Bible, consider using a different translation that's easier to read or an audiobook Bible that allows you to listen to God's Word wherever you are.

1. What role does reading the Bible play in your spiritual life?

2. On the continuum below, mark the ease or difficulty you face in your attempt to read the Bible every day.

I find reading
the Bible every
day easy.

I struggle to
read the Bible
every day.

3. On the continuum below, mark the ease or difficulty you face in relating what you read in the Bible to your life.

I often find what I
read in the Bible
speaks into the
situations I face.

I rarely find what
I read in the Bible
speaks into the
situations I face.

Paul served as a voice of encouragement and as a spiritual mentor to Timothy. In 2 Timothy 3, Paul warned Timothy difficult times would come.

4. **Read 2 Timothy 3:1–15**. Which of the things Paul described have you seen or experienced in our modern world? What did Paul encourage Timothy to do in response (hint: verses 14, 15)?

5. **Read 2 Timothy 3:16, 17.** In the space below, make a list of the four ways Paul gave that Scripture is beneficial. When have you experienced God using the Bible to do each one of these in your life?

Benefits of Scripture	How I've Experienced This in My Life
1	
2	
3	
4	

6. What does Scripture prepare us for according to 2 Timothy 3:17? When have you experienced this passage to be true in your life?

One of the most important things when reading the Bible is our attitude. If we approach Scripture with the mind-set that it's going to be difficult to read, irrelevant to our lives, or something we need to check off our spiritual to-do lists, then we're probably not going to get much out of it. But if we open God's Word with an attitude of divine expectation, humble prayer, and wide-eyed eagerness, then we're prepared and available for God to speak, lead, and guide us.

7. **Read John 14:26 and 1 Corinthians 2:10–14**. What role does the Holy Spirit play as you read the Bible? Have you ever taken the time to ask the Holy Spirit to open up the Scripture before you begin reading? If so, what difference did this make?

8. **Read Psalm 119:103**. How can you begin developing a sweet tooth for God's Word?

Digging Deeper

The longest chapter of the Bible, Psalm 119, is considered a Torah psalm because every verse refers to Scripture. **Read Psalm 119:11**. How have you experienced transformation while reading, studying, and obeying the Bible? How does spending time in the Scripture affect your attitude and approach toward life? When was the last time you felt compelled to do something or not do something because of a passage you read or studied? What prevents you from spending more time reading and reflecting on Scripture?

✣ Personal Challenge

Commit to reading at least one chapter of the Bible each day this week. If you're not sure where to begin, consider reading in Psalms or one of the Gospels, such as John. Before you read, spend time preparing your heart, mind, and spirit. Ask God to give a sense of expectation for what He wants to reveal. Ask the Holy Spirit to illuminate the passage and raise your awareness of particular words, phrases, or ideas. Ask God to make Scripture alive and vibrant, revealing His heart to you as you read. Open God's Word expectant for how God may choose to answer.

"God's story does not end with the return of chaos. Instead, he began a long process of restoring harmony to his creation. What is truly amazing is that he chose to accomplish this process in partnership with people—the same created beings who had ruined it in the first place! He commands his created human beings to live lives that bring harmony to his creation and forbids whatever causes brokenness or prevents the restoration he desires."

Ray Vander Laan,
minister and teacher[1]

The Law

A Portrait of the Character and Heart of God

Imagine cracking open a law book and reading the volume from beginning to end. You'd probably discover many laws and edicts you've never considered, rulings on situations you never thought possible.

Sometimes this is what reading through the Old Testament law, as contained in the books of Exodus, Leviticus, Numbers, and Deuteronomy, can feel like. Some of the more than six hundred laws recorded in these books may seem odd at first glance. For example, Numbers 15:38 commands, "Speak to the children of Israel: Tell them to make tassels on the corners of their garments throughout their generations, and to put a blue thread in the tassels of the corners."

Now that's a lot of tassels! Why would God command this? The next verse explains, "And you shall have the tassel, that you may look upon it and remember all the commandments of the LORD and do them." In other words, the sight of these tassels was a reminder to obey God. To this day, Orthodox Jews wear prayer shawls that feature these tassels.

Many of the laws found in the Old Testament addressed situations and ways of life foreign to us in the twenty-first century. For example, Leviticus 19:27 instructs men not to clip the hair from their temples or beards, and Leviticus 11:6–8 says that touching the skin of a dead pig will make you unclean. Such passages can lead a modern reader to wonder, "But what if my son wants to grow a goatee or play football in the backyard?"

> Many of the laws are non-applicable or irrelevant to us today, so don't worry . . .

This is when it's important to remember that the Old Testament law was never given as a means for salvation—that was accomplished through Jesus Christ alone. When you read the Old Testament law, know it's the basis of the old covenant—the rules God established for His chosen people. Because of the new covenant given through Christ's sacrifice on the cross, the law is not binding to Christians, except where explicitly stated in the New Testament.

Many of the laws are non-applicable or irrelevant to us today, so don't worry: your son can grow a goatee and toss a football. However, a few of the laws have been renewed.

When someone asked Jesus which was the most important law in the Bible, He said, "'You shall love the LORD your God with all your heart, with all your soul, and with all your mind.' This is *the* first and great commandment. And *the* second *is* like it: 'You shall love your neighbor as yourself.' On these two commandments hang all the Law and the Prophets" (Matthew 22:37–40).

Jesus hand-selected Deuteronomy 6:5 and Leviticus 19:18 as two laws from the Old Testament that remain. The call to love God and love others is timeless. In addition, the Ten Commandments are also referred to throughout the New Testament (Matthew 5:21–37; John 7:23).

So if we don't have to obey the hundreds of laws, then why is reading the law still important? Because it reveals wondrous truths about God.

The law isn't given to arbitrarily limit freedom, but to guide, protect, and bless God's people. Through the law, we get to glimpse God's incredible love, intricate involvement, and plans for His people. By studying the law, we also see God's desire to make His people holy. We see what showing loyalty to God above all else looks like. Studying the law also exposes our own sinfulness and reveals how much we need Christ.

Reading through the Old Testament law provides a window into the lifestyle and culture of ancient Israel. Because much of the world the Israelites lived in is foreign to us, picking up a study Bible can be helpful. These types of Bibles contain many bonus features—notes, observations, historical and cultural backgrounds, and more.

Old Testament law called God's chosen people, the Israelites, to love one another in every area of life—even in their work. The law constantly challenged people to walk in greater levels of integrity, kindness, love, forgiveness, generosity, and grace with each other as they followed God.

✤ Three Things to Remember

- The law wasn't given to take away freedom as much as to empower God's people to walk in true freedom and holiness. When followed, the law brought much blessing to the people of Israel.

- The Old Testament law is the basis of the old covenant and Israel's history, but isn't binding on Christians, except where renewed in the New Testament such as the Ten Commandments, loving God, and loving others.

- When interpreting Old Testament law, keep a commentary or study Bible nearby to shed light onto cultural nuances that we, as modern-day readers, may not understand.

1. **Read Leviticus 19:9, 10**. What does God command in this passage? What does the command reveal about God's concern for the poor and foreigner? What's one way you can demonstrate this kind of care for others in your life right now?

2. **Read Leviticus 19:11–18**. What does God command in this passage? What are some of the practical outcomes of obeying these laws? What do these laws reveal about God's heart for His people?

The Old Testament law reveals God's concern with all kinds of details—how the people treated each other, animals, and the land. Some of the laws even focused on people's diets. Several passages in the Old Testament law, including Leviticus 11 and Deuteronomy 14, list foods to be eaten and others to be avoided.

3. **Read Leviticus 11:1–25**. In the space below, draw pictures of a few animals the Israelites were forbidden to eat within this passage. Which of the animals listed would be hardest for you to avoid? Which of the animals listed would be easiest for you to avoid?

Scholars note such food laws weren't meant to limit the diets of Israelites but were for protective purposes. The majority of prohibited foods were more likely to carry diseases. In addition, many of the foods were uneconomical or unreasonable to raise in the region. Some of the foods were forbidden because they were popular among religious groups the Israelites were not to duplicate. Modern scientists have pointed out that the main source of Israel's meat, lamb, is the least allergenic of all major meat sources.[2]

The Old Testament law provided something that no other nation had—a covenant or agreement between God and the people. Receiving the law was meant to be a source of blessing for God's people—a sign that He was committed to them and, through obedience, they were committed to Him. Through Christ, the law was fulfilled, ushering in the new covenant, but the Ten Commandments still appeared in the New Testament.

4. Fill in the following chart of commandments and how they are referenced in the New Testament.

Old Testament References	Commandment	New Testament References	How are they referenced?
Exodus 20:2, 3		Matthew 4:10; 6:24	
Exodus 20:4–6		1 John 5:21; 1 Corinthians 10:7	
Exodus 20:7		Matthew 6:9; 1 Timothy 6:1	

Old Testament References	Commandment	New Testament References	How are they referenced?
Exodus 20:8–11		Matthew 12:8, 12; Hebrews 4:9	
Exodus 20:12		Matthew 15:3, 4; 19:19; Ephesians 6:1–3	
Exodus 20:13		Matthew 5:21, 22; Romans 13:9	
Exodus 20:14		Matthew 5:27, 28	
Exodus 20:15		Matthew 19:18; Ephesians 4:28	
Exodus 20:16		Matthew 12:36, 37; 19:18	
Exodus 20:17		Luke 12:15; 1 Timothy 6:10	

5. What is the focus of the first four commandments in Exodus 20:2–11?

6. What is the focus of the last six commandments in Exodus 20:12–17?

7. Which of these commandments challenges you to love God more? Which of these commandments challenges you to love others more? Which of these commandments challenges you to do both?

8. **Read Galatians 3:24**. According to this passage, what is the purpose of the law? How do the Ten Commandments fulfill this purpose? How does reading and reflecting on the law challenge you to become a more committed follower of Jesus?

Digging Deeper

God wasn't making a list of dos and don'ts just for fun—He had a plan to bless and prosper the Israelites. But choosing to disobey also carried consequences. **Read Leviticus 26:1–46**. How did God desire to bless His people for their obedience? What was their punishment for disobedience? How does reflecting on this passage affect your desire to obey God?

✣ Personal Challenge

Pick up a Bible and read Deuteronomy 6:4–9. Make a list of five different ways you can become more intentional about reading, sharing, and memorizing Scripture. Do one of them each day this week. Be creative! Share your ideas with the group the next time you meet.

"It is our presupposition that the Holy Spirit knew what He was doing when He inspired so much of the Bible in the form of narrative. We think it is obvious that this type of literature serves God's revelatory purpose well."

Gordon D. Fee and Douglas Stuart,
Bible professors[1]

Narrative History
Grasping the Big Story of God

If any writing style is most common in the Bible, it's narrative history. If you flip open your Bible, particularly the first half of the book, there's a good chance you're going to open to a page with narrative history. Scholars estimate biblical narrative stories compose 40 percent of the Old Testament and quite a bit of the New Testament.

So what is narrative history? It's simply the stories of what happened to God's people. Some of the stories tell of mind-bending, unimaginable adventures. Others are like well-paced, whodunit mysteries. Still others are slowly unfolding tales that lead to the unexpected aha! moment.

This wildly compelling narrative fills the pages of Genesis, Joshua, Judges, Ruth, 1 and 2 Samuel, 1 and 2 Kings, 1 and 2 Chronicles, Ezra, Nehemiah, Esther, and Jonah. You'll find rich narrative among the likes of Daniel, Haggai, Exodus, Numbers,

Jeremiah, Ezekiel, Isaiah, and Job. The page-turning storytelling continues throughout many of the four Gospels and almost all of Acts.

Through accounts of imprisonment and coronation, storms and shipwrecks, we read the harrowing adventures of those who have chosen to follow God. But these stories are always pointing to something, or rather Someone, greater. Through historical narrative we better understand God and ourselves as we see how people responded to God in unique situations and circumstances throughout the years. These stories help us grasp the character of God, His likes and dislikes, and His longing for relationship with us—even when we make huge mistakes.

Behind every ploy twist and developing event, God is at work as the most decisive character of all.

While some narrative stories provide great models of how to handle a situation, often they do just the opposite—demonstrating exactly what we should not do. Remember when Jonah hitchhiked a water taxi to avoid going to Nineveh?

Sometimes the teaching is explicit or clearly stated, but sometimes not. Meaning can be discovered or affirmed by reading another part of the Bible. Remember the love story of Ruth and Boaz as a representation of God's love for us?

Whenever we read a narrative—some will make us laugh, cry, and even sigh—the real story is always about God. Behind every plot twist and developing event, God is at work as the most decisive character of all.

Sometimes biblical narrative will go to great depths, sharing every detail of an encounter or scene, followed by years of silence. The stark contrast leaves every reader wanting. We *want* someone to fill in the blanks. We *want* someone to tell us what we long to know. But this isn't the Bible's purpose.

Narratives aren't written to give us every last detail or answer every last question about an issue. They point to the greater work God is doing throughout history. If we read between the lines too much, we'll find ourselves writing things into the story that simply aren't there. God gave us the Bible not so that we could find what we wanted to hear or know, but so He could share what He wanted to say.

As we savor narratives of heroes and foes throughout the Bible, remember that most of the teaching isn't direct, but implied. The stories were written to show not what should have happened but what did happen. Not every story will have a moral, but it will reveal something about God being the Hero to us all.

✤ Three Things to Remember

- God is the author behind every story.

- Biblical narratives weren't written to describe every last detail and answer every question. Instead, they focus on what God is doing throughout history.

- Narrative history in the Old Testament describes the lives of the Israelites—God's chosen people.

1. Below is a list of ten people from the Bible whose stories are often told through historical narrative. Whose story do you relate to most? Explain.

Joseph (Genesis 37—50)	Samuel (1 Samuel 1)
Moses (Exodus)	Joshua (Joshua)
David (1 and 2 Samuel; 1 Kings; 1 Chronicles)	Esther (Esther)
Jonah (Jonah)	Nehemiah (Nehemiah)
Ruth (Ruth)	Paul (Acts 7:54—8:3; 1-31, 13-28)

2. Reflecting on the person you relate to most, what particular moments or details from his or her journey endeared you to this person?

3. What has this person taught you that has been most encouraging as you follow Christ?

4. **Read 2 Samuel 11:1–4**. If you only read and knew this part of the story, what kind of conclusions could you draw from the historical narrative? How would you be shortchanged? Why is reading the entire story of David's life important?

5. **Read 2 Samuel 11:5–27**. Why do you think this passage concludes with what God thinks about the situation?

6. Why is God's perspective on this story and every other story you read in Scripture important?

7. **Read 2 Samuel 12:1–25**. What does this narrative reveal about God's judgment? What does this narrative reveal about God's faithfulness?

8. Who is the hero of this narrative? What does this narrative reveal about God's love?

Digging Deeper

One of the most moving stories in Scripture is the account of Joseph, who rose from prison to palace. **Read Genesis 37—50**. What does Joseph's story reveal about God's plan and purposes? What does Joseph's story reveal about God's goodness in difficult circumstances? How does Joseph's story encourage you in the situation you're currently facing?

✤ Personal Challenge

Throughout the upcoming week, practice reading the great big story of God by diving into 1 Kings. Commit to reading at least three chapters a day. With each passing page, imagine you're reading it as if for the first time. Place question marks by unfamiliar passages. Ask God to illuminate details. Allow the story to capture your imagination as you prayerfully consider the words.

"Wisdom is as much about seeing clearly as it is about making decisions and acting. To do what is right, one must be able to discern what the good is in a variety of situations, and wisdom promises to teach how that may be done."

Paul E. Koptak,
biblical scholar[1]

Wisdom Literature
Living the Best Possible Life

Have you ever found yourself caught in a sticky situation and were unsure of what to do? All of us have! And this is why the wisdom literature is such a great source of guidance in our lives. Wisdom literature—which includes books such as Job, Ecclesiastes, Proverbs, Song of Solomon, and a handful of psalms—is filled with God-centered guidance for everyday life.

Throughout these books, we find wisdom on how to parent, handle finances, maintain healthy relationships, and so much more. We also receive warnings on those things that can draw us away from God and each other—like pride, selfishness, unforgiveness, and gossip. Some of the teachings are common sense; others carry a poetic sagacity and sophistication.

Wisdom literature doesn't back down when asking the tough questions of life, many of which don't have ready-made answers. Passages in Job, Ecclesiastes, and the Psalms ask questions about

God, humanity, suffering, good, and evil. In this genre, few topics are off limits. This type of literature asks why good things happen to bad people and why bad things happen to good people. Through the story of Job, we discover there isn't a simple or easy answer to such questions. Rather, comfort is found in God's presence and sovereignty.

Reading this genre invites all of us to walk in greater discernment and understanding. Followers of God are called to live with discretion, prudence, self-control, and grace, and to avoid the paths of folly. Proverbs offers tips and tidbits, insights and information on making the best possible choices in life.

Sometimes wisdom literature can be a little tricky to understand. Passages from the book of Ecclesiastes can feel cynical and downright depressing. Consider the book's opening declaration: "'Vanity of vanities,' says the Preacher; 'Vanity of vanities, all *is* vanity'" (Ecclesiastes 1:2). Yet further reading reveals everything does feel meaningless if one chooses to live a life outside of obedience to God. Like every genre of literature in the Bible, context really matters.

One of the greatest gifts of wisdom literature is, through the writing, we're reminded the topics and issues the Israelites wrestled with thousands of years ago aren't too different from our own. Just as they struggled with questions of sin and suffering, we do too. Just as they experienced doubt and fears, we do too. Just as they searched for God in the midst of life's triumphs and tragedies, we do too. And just as God treasured and responded to their honest heart cries and prayers, He responds to us too.

Sometimes wisdom literature can be a little tricky to understand.

✤ Three Things to Remember:

- A proverb is a short saying easily remembered and recognized.

- The theme of "the fear of God" is commonly found in wisdom literature. It is the idea that our knowledge of God draws us near to Him, yet makes us stand in awe.

- When reading proverbs, remember they are written to be practical (not theological), interpreted with historical context, and are meant to be guidelines rather than guarantees.

1. In the midst of your everyday, where do you tend to turn for wisdom?

2. Describe a time when you found the wisdom you needed from the Bible. What passage was particularly helpful for you during this time?

Wisdom enables us to make choices in life that are glorifying to God and help transform us into the image of Christ. Wisdom is concerned not with collecting more information, but with how to learn to make decisions producing the desired results that are naturally God honoring. Wisdom calls to us if we have ears to hear.

The book of Proverbs has more than one author. It is an anthology of wise sayings collected during the time of King Solomon. While Solomon, known for his wisdom, probably didn't write the majority of Proverbs, he read and heeded each of these proverbs—which led to his renowned wisdom.

3. **Read Proverbs 1:1–7**. Where does wisdom originate? According to this passage, how are proverbs helpful to you? What are you supposed to learn from all these tidbits of wisdom?

4. **Read Proverbs 1:8–19**. What entices you to not walk in wisdom? What are results of choosing this path?

Proverbs 1 describes the female personification of God's wisdom—*Sophia* in Greek. Sophia calls out to readers, inviting us to listen and learn from her.

5. **Read Proverbs 1:20–33**. What are the warnings in this passage for those who refuse to walk in wisdom? What are the rewards of those who choose this path (hint: verse 33)? How have you seen what this passage describes to be true in your life?

Wisdom is a priceless treasure carrying great rewards. The authors of Proverbs encourage readers to give up the self-centered life and hold tight to wisdom—a God-centered life.

6. **Read Proverbs 3:1–12**. In the space below, make a list of the rewards of those who choose to walk in wisdom. Circle the reward most meaningful to you right now.

Even the New Testament speaks of the importance of wisdom. James reminds us wisdom is needed in the Christian's life to live according to God's purpose and plan. Wisdom empowers us to see life through God's perspective.

7. **Read James 1:5**. What is the secret to gaining wisdom? What prevents you from gaining more wisdom every day?

8. In the space below, make a list of three situations or areas of your life in which you need God's wisdom. Then spend time praying and asking God to give you wisdom in each area.

Digging Deeper

Read Proverbs 19. Which of these proverbs are most meaningful for you today? Why? In what ways are proverbs highly practical? What do proverbs emphasize about how we live our lives?

✤ Personal Challenge

Ecclesiastes can be a tough book of the Bible to read if you don't understand what it's trying to communicate. The vast majority of the book is an argument of how one would view life and the world if God weren't active and intimately involved. The book shows the disappointment and heartache that comes while trying to live life while keeping God at arm's distance. Over the course of the next week, read Ecclesiastes with the help of a study Bible or commentary to better understand this challenging book of the Bible.

"The Psalms model ways of talking to God that are honest, yet not obvious—at least, they are not obvious to modern Christians. They may guide our first steps toward deeper involvement with God, because the Psalms give us new possibility for prayer; they invite full disclosure."

Ellen F. Davis,
Bible scholar[1]

The Psalms

Timeless Songs and Prayers for Every Age

Some of the most beautiful writing in the entire Bible is found in the Psalms. King David and many others expressed their joys, heartaches, doubts, and declarations to God through a rich collection of songs, hymns, and prayers.

Within ancient culture, poetry was celebrated and appreciated. This type of literature was often easier to memorize than traditional prose. The rhythm, cadence, and repetition made the refrains memorable. Unlike straightforward writing, poetry contains an ability to not only speak to the mind but captivate the heart. The words of the poet are often penetrating and haunting. Long after the song or prayer has ended, the syllables still swing in our spirits.

Hebrew poetry often uses parallelism, in which the author makes the same point with different words. Sometimes the psalmist accomplishes this by contrasting the first line with the second; other times he does this by stating the same idea twice. Consider the opening of Psalm 1:1, 2:

> Blessed *is* the man
> Who walks not in the counsel of the ungodly,
> Nor stands in the path of sinners,
> Nor sits in the seat of the scornful;
> But his delight *is* in the law of the LORD,
> And in His law he meditates day and night.

Such poetry isn't based on rhyme or meter as much as the repetitive nature of the words and ideas. Thus, Hebrew poetry transcends translation—its beauty and breadth is displayed in every language.

Throughout the Psalms you'll find all kinds of different categories or types of musical poems including laments, hymns of praise, songs of thanksgiving, royal psalms, pilgrimage psalms, and more. Though the Psalms point us to God and truths about Him, we cannot read a psalm as we would a theological treatise or doctrine. We need to remember emotions, vivid imagery, and even exaggeration in the form of hyperbole are used to express the poet's heart cry.

We can turn to the Psalms to find guidance as we worship, praise, and pray.

The Psalms are powerful reminders that we can express our hearts wholly and fully to God and know He hears us. We can turn to the Psalms to find guidance as we worship, praise, and pray. We can turn to the Psalms in times of need that leave us speechless. We can turn to the Psalms to remember that God welcomes our honesty. And we can turn to the Psalms as we reflect on the goodness and faithfulness of God to provide, deliver, and remain ever-present. Indeed, the Psalms remind us it's in the presence of God we can be transformed forever.

✤ Three Things to Remember

- Ancient Hebrew poetry contains little to no rhyme.
- Hebrew poetry often uses word pairs, rhythm, unusual word order and vocabulary, and figurative language.
- The book of Psalms includes poems and songs in these categories: hymn, thanksgiving, lament, imprecatory, wisdom, Torah, and royal.

Oftentimes, the psalmist used language and word pictures as a form of praise to God. This technique is called a hymn psalm. Psalm 8 describes breathtaking beauty and delight in God's creation and character. It begins and ends with the same refrain, a repetition of praise—even God's name, Yahweh, is majestic.

1. **Read Psalm 8**. How does God display His splendor?

2. **Read Matthew 21:15, 16**. How does Jesus' statement affirm Psalm 8:2?

God is both transcendent (wholly different and distinct) and immanent (close and near) to humanity. The combination is an incomprehensible paradox—one to be praised and celebrated.

3. What observations did the psalmist make about humanity in each of the following verses:

Psalm 8:2:

Psalm 8:3, 4:

Psalm 8:5–8:

How does meditating on the splendors of God affect the psalmist's perspective on humanity?

4. Do you tend to center your life around bringing glory to yourself or to God? How does this psalm challenge the way you see yourself? Others? God?

One type of psalm is known as lament. Lament psalms are the most common group of psalms. They are prayerful songs that express pain, suffering, struggles, and challenges, which at times seem insurmountable. Some laments are personal, but others are an expression of a group of people. Lament gives us the opportunity to turn our pain into praise, our tears into joy.

5. **Read Psalm 3**. Which of the following elements do you see displayed in this passage? Place a check mark by each one.

_____ An invocation for God

_____ A complaint of distress

_____ A petition for intervention or vengeance

_____ A confession of sin or proclamation of innocence

_____ A vow of praise to God for deliverance

_____ An expression of trust in God

_____ A final praise

6. Despite the taunts of his enemies who said God wouldn't come to his rescue, the psalmist chose to place trust in God. When have you been challenged recently to place your trust in God despite opposition?

7. What is one area of your life where you are currently struggling or have experienced loss or pain? Take what you're thinking and feeling to God in the form of lament. Write your own lament psalm to God in the space below using the following cues. (If you need another reference for lament, read Psalms 22 or 39.)

An invocation for God	
A complaint of distress	
A petition for intervention or vengeance	
A confession of sin or proclamation of innocence	
A vow of praise to God for deliverance	
An expression of trust in God	
A final praise	

8. When have you tried to hold back your emotions and honest thoughts from God in the past? What freedom do you experience when you're honest with God through lament?

Digging Deeper

The Israelites used psalms as part of worship. **Read Psalm 47 and Psalm 93**. Both were used to celebrate the enthronement of God as King and were considered royal psalms. What common elements do you see in the two psalms? What kind of emotion is expressed through these psalms? In your life, where do you struggle to make God King and give Him full reign?

✣ Personal Challenge

Commit to reading at least one psalm each day this week. If you're able, consider reading two or three each day. Don't forget to take time before you read to prepare your heart, mind, and spirit. Ask God to make the Scripture alive and vibrant as you read. Look for portions of psalms or entire chapters you can pray aloud to God.

"The prophets and the writers of the Psalms were clear that God was continuing to work in the universe and in all history. They declared that He had created the universe."

Kenneth Scott Latourette,
historian[1]

The Prophets

Calling People to Love God and Others

Consider the following riddle:

> What always runs but never walks?
> What often murmurs but never talks?
> What has a bed but never sleeps?
> What has a mouth but never eats?

Can you feel your brain twisting and maybe even flipping summersaults to land on the right answer? If you knew or read the answer right now, the riddle would make perfect sense.

Every line. Every word.

You'd smile from ear to ear.

Those who listened to the prophets of the Old Testament likely felt similar emotions. From the groping to the joy of comprehension, those who heard the four major prophets—Isaiah, Jeremiah, Ezekiel, and Daniel—as well as the twelve minor prophets—Hosea, Joel, Amos, Obadiah, Jonah, Micah, Nahum, Habakkuk, Zephaniah, Haggai, Zechariah, and Malachi—often struggled to wrap their minds and hearts around what they were hearing.

At times, the prophets spoke clearly and concisely in words everyone could understand. But other times they turned to imagery and prophetic actions far more difficult to comprehend. Oftentimes, people misunderstood the prophets to be announcing events in the distant future when they were speaking of the immediate future of God's people and the surrounding nations. Little surprise the prophetic books are among the toughest to read, interpret, and apply.

> At times, the prophets spoke clearly and concisely in words everyone could understand.

This is why looking for additional help when reading the prophets is important. Picking up a Bible dictionary will help you understand hard-to-pronounce words and odd-sounding imagery. A commentary can be a great resource too. These books provide lengthy introductions and detailed explanations of individual verses.

For some prophets, such as Elijah, Elisha, and Jonah, we read far more about their journeys and lives than what they actually declared from God. But other prophets, such as Ezekiel, offer colorful prophetic images often shrouded in mystery.

Most of the prophets offer a few common elements in their messages: an expression of Israel's sin and/or God's unfathomable love for her as well as the prediction of blessing or curse based on the circumstances and response. In essence, the prophets were kind of like Covenant Enforcement Officers. They were the ones God chose to remind people of the covenant they'd made as followers of God. Sometimes, the prophets reminded the people of the countless blessings from upholding the covenant.

Other times, the prophets delivered hard news of the punishment or consequences from breaking the covenant. And sometimes the prophets delivered news of what was yet to come—like the promise of Christ.

The prophets ground us in our commitment to God and call us back to holiness when we go astray. They anchor us in God's tremendous love and commitment to us.

✣ Three Things to Remember

- The prophets remind us of God's covenant or promises and unending love for His people.

- Prophets usually spoke bad news. The book of Jeremiah offers a rule of thumb when determining a true prophet: prophets who prophesy peace will be of the Lord if the prediction comes true (Jeremiah 28:9).

- Many passages in prophetic literature have a deeper meaning intended by God, but not intended by the human author.

1. How did you respond to the riddle at the beginning of this lesson? What did the riddle make you think, feel, and reflect on? (The riddle's answer is in the back of the study.)

2. How do you tend to respond while reading the prophets? Mark all that apply. Then explain your answer.

_____ Intrigued   _____ Overwhelmed

_____ Excited   _____ Confused

_____ Surprised   _____ Frustrated

_____ Amazed   _____ Indifferent

_____ Shocked   _____ Other

Ezekiel is considered a major prophet. The main difference between a major prophet and a minor prophet in the Old Testament isn't based on the prophet's importance or the potency of his message, but rather the length of the book. The long-winded are known as major prophets, and the more concise are known as minor prophets.

God chose Ezekiel to warn the Jews living in Babylon to confess their sin and turn back to God. Almost halfway through the book of Ezekiel, the prophet's predictions made a dramatic shift from scary images of judgment to the hope-filled plans God had for Israel.

3. **Read Ezekiel 37:1–14**. Draw a picture of what's described in this passage in the space below.

Scholars suggest the valley imagery is more than a geographical location. It's representative of the people living in exile who have been removed from the high mountain of their homeland of Israel. This is a place of pain, loss, and death, and the people must be delivered, but God alone can deliver them.

4. What does God ask Ezekiel in Ezekiel 37:3? How does Ezekiel respond? What does the question reveal about God and Ezekiel?

5. What role does Ezekiel play in bringing the bones back to life in Ezekiel 37:4–14? How do you think the story might have ended differently if Ezekiel hadn't responded in obedience?

The vision is a word of encouragement to the Israelites that though their future looks desolate, nothing is beyond God's commitment to save and restore His people.

This Old Testament prophecy contains rich imagery offering an opportunity for personal reflection and inventory.

6. When have you felt like the pile of dry bones in your spiritual life? What or who did God use to breathe His life into you?

The prophet Isaiah used imagery to reveal a promise of hope and life to those who are afflicted, which Jesus fulfilled in the New Testament. Old Testament prophecy often revealed foretelling. Foretelling is the ability to see the foothills but not the mountains. Isaiah foretold hope for the afflicted in his time. The New Testament authors, such as Matthew, were able to look back with forthtelling. Forthtelling is the ability to look back and see both the foothills and the mountains. Matthew was able to look back in history and see how Christ fulfilled Isaiah's prophecy.

7. **Read Isaiah 61:1-3 and Matthew 3:16**. What parallels do you see between the liberty and life declared in these passages and the work of God displayed in Ezekiel 37:1-14?

8. Who in your life looks like a pile of dry bones or is held captive or brokenhearted right now? Which of these people do you sense God asking you to breathe His life and love into his or her life?

Digging Deeper

Isaiah contains four passages known as the Suffering Servant songs (Isaiah 42:1-9; 49:1-6; 50:4-9; 52:13—53:12). These songs describe God's Servant who is coming to embody God's power, bear others' suffering, and fulfill God's will. The fulfillment of the Suffering Servant is Christ. **Read Isaiah 52:13—53:12**. What are the characteristics of the Servant? How well does this passage predict the life of Christ?

✤ Personal Challenge

Amos was a minor prophet with a major message. He called God's people to integrity, to justice, and to care for those in need. He reminded the Jews to love God and others above all else and let their lives reflect that love. But if they didn't, judgment would come to the land in the form of foreign military forces that would overtake the kingdom. During the upcoming week, grab a study Bible and commentary and read the book of Amos to learn more about this shepherd-turned-prophet.

Sampling the New Testament Genres

Some of the genres we'll look at in the second half of the study are unique to the New Testament, such as the Gospels. Others are contained in the Old and New Testaments, such as genealogies. All give us greater insights into God and His tender care for us.

"The gospel is not a doctrine of the tongue, but of life. It cannot be grasped by reason and memory only, but it is fully understood when it possesses the whole soul and penetrates to the inner recesses of the heart."

John Calvin,
French reformer and theologian[1]

The Gospels
Falling in Love with Jesus

Gospel **means "good news,"** and the great news available to all of us is salvation through Jesus Christ. But who is this man Jesus? What did He teach? How did He interact with people?

The four Gospels—Matthew, Mark, Luke, and John—all offer different portraits of the life and ministry of Jesus Christ. Like a princess-cut diamond, they all reflect different perspectives and details of the life of Jesus, and each one is incredibly beautiful.

Reading the Gospels is like sitting down with a group of old friends remembering a shared experience. Though everyone encountered the same things, each person recalls different details and has a unique perspective.

Matthew was a detail-oriented kind of guy. He loved to go into great depth and detail about the life and ministry of Christ. Matthew was committed to proving Jesus was the promised Messiah. In fact, he used the phrase (or one similar) "that it might be fulfilled which was spoken by prophet" ten times in his book. To accomplish this, he traced the lineage of Jesus to David and quoted lots of Old Testament passages to show Jesus fulfilled the words of the prophets. Throughout Matthew, you'll find lots of references to Jewish customs. When telling the story of Jesus, Matthew tended to organize the facts by subject matter rather than exact linear or calendar time.

Mark wrote to non-Jewish believers in Rome who weren't familiar with Jewish customs or Old Testament prophecy. So Mark's account is filled with the works of Christ. He was a much more brief and concise storyteller who loved to use the word *immediately* and lots of active verbs budding with anticipation. While Matthew sought to establish Christ as King and long-awaited Messiah, Mark portrayed Christ as Servant and Savior of the world. Rather than a genealogy, Mark began with Jesus' story of public ministry. He showed Jesus demonstrating compassion, meeting the physical and spiritual needs of the people.

Luke is the longest of the Gospels and serves as the first of a two-part series that continues in Acts. Luke addressed his writing to Theophilus, a Gentile, so the original audience was Greek. Luke tied Jesus' family tree all the way back to Adam in order to show God's love reached all of humanity—even those who weren't Jewish. As a physician, Luke brought a unique perspective to the story of Christ. He noted details—such as the miracles surrounding Christ's birth—other gospels didn't include. Luke recorded spectacular details about the healings of Jesus. His account reminds us Jesus always had an eye for those on the margins—the widows, children, women, and Samaritans.

John is the most colorful of all the Gospel writers. Writing to new Christians, many of whom were being persecuted for their faith, John began with a portion of cosmic poetry linking Christ's arrival with the

> As a physician, Luke brought a unique perspective to the story of Christ.

story of creation. John told stories that don't appear in the other gospels—like when Jesus saved a wedding by turning water into wine and when He raised one of His close friends, Lazarus, from the dead. John wrote so people would believe Jesus was the Christ, the Son of God, and experience the love of God for themselves.

Together the Gospels tell us about the birth, life, ministry, death, and resurrection of Jesus. Through the writing of Matthew, Mark, Luke, and John, we don't just discover what Jesus did but who Jesus is—the Son of God. We learn of His passion, His priorities, His humanness, and His sacrifice. These writings invite us to fall in love with Jesus again and again.

✤ Three Things to Remember

- The Gospels are four different eyewitness accounts of Jesus' life, ministry, death, and resurrection. Because of this, each author has a fresh perspective, which accounts for why some details may be slightly different from book to book.

- When reading and studying the Gospels, keep in mind each author wrote to a specific audience, which affects the language, characters, setting, and focus. Matthew's gospel was written to a Jewish audience. Mark's gospel was written to a Roman audience. Luke's gospel was written for a Greek or Gentile audience. John's gospel was universally written.

- Many Bible translations print the words of Jesus in red. These red letters help us recognize what Jesus said.

Matthew, a Jewish tax collector, focused his gospel on God's promised kingdom brought to earth. Over the course of his gospel, he describes how Jesus fulfilled the law and promises of God. He refers to Jesus as the

Son of David—supporting Jesus' legal right to the throne, and the Son of Abraham—supporting Jesus' ethnic right to the throne.

1. **Read Matthew 1:18—2:12**. Look up each of the following passages. How are each of the following prophecies fulfilled through Christ's birth?

Passage	Fulfillment in Matthew
Isaiah 7:14	
Isaiah 60:3	
Isaiah 62:11	
Micah 5:2	

2. How does reflecting on the prophecies Jesus fulfilled strengthen your faith? How does seeing God's fulfilled promises in Christ give you hope that God will fulfill His promises to you?

Mark studied with Jesus' disciple Peter and records Jesus' life with a pastoral and practical perspective. Mark was an action-packed storyteller. He didn't waste a word, but pre-loaded his accounts with a great expectation of just-what-might-happen-next.

Mark 5 introduces us to two bold and faith-filled characters. One is a woman who suffers physically, socially, and spiritually from an ailment. The other is a man named Jairus who flagged Jesus' attention on behalf of his dying daughter. With the exception of the disciples, Jairus is one of the few characters in Mark's gospel given a name.

Both stories remind us that no matter our wealth or stature, faith enables us all to tap into Jesus' healing power.

3. **Read Mark 5:21–43**. In the space below, make a list of all Jesus does in this passage. How many times does the word "immediately" appear?

4. What does this passage from Mark reveal about turning to Jesus for healing and salvation?

The author of Luke compiled evidence of Jesus' life into the historical and chronological gospel of Luke, written around AD 85. Many scholars believe the author of this gospel to be Luke the physician (Colossians 4:14). Luke shares stories from the life of Jesus that aren't told in any other gospel—many which focus on salvation and the marginalized.

5. Below is a list of stories unique to Luke. What do you think these stories reveal about Christ's love and compassion for those who are marginalized?

The Good Samaritan (Luke 10:25–37)
The Friend at Midnight (Luke 11:5–8)
The Lost Coin (Luke 15:8–10)
The Prodigal Son (Luke 15:11–32)
The Rich Man and Lazarus (Luke 16:19–31)

6. What changes do you need to make in your life to expand your capacity to see and embrace those on the margins?

    The mention of *life* appears in John's gospel more than any other book in the entire New Testament. John invites people to believe in Jesus and the eternal life given by God's Son. John begins his gospel with a rich blend of theology and poetry. Instead of beginning with genealogy or an argument, he paints a portrait of God incarnate in the person of Jesus Christ.

7. **Read John 1:1–18**. What does John's introduction reveal about his purpose for writing? What questions about Jesus does this passage raise for you?

8. Reflecting on the four gospel writers, which approach to telling the story of Jesus appeals to your own personality and learning style? Why?

Digging Deeper

One way to distinguish between the Gospels is by studying the way each one begins. **Read Matthew 1, Mark 1, Luke 1, and John 1**. What are the gospel writers trying to accomplish through their writing? Which approach is easiest for you to connect with? Which is the most difficult for you to connect with? What can you gain by studying and reading each one?

✤ Personal Challenge

One of the great gifts of the Gospels is that we are able to read and study what Jesus said. Often the words of Jesus are marked in red in Bibles. This week, consider taking one of the Gospels, such as Mark, and simply read through the words Jesus said. Prayerfully consider what Jesus is saying to you through these passages.

"In Jesus God's promises in the Old Testament have come true."

Grant R. Osborne,
New Testament professor[1]

Genealogies
Hidden Treasures of the Bible

When we find genealogies, allowing our eyes to glaze over is all too easy. We may find ourselves stumbling and fumbling through lists of hard-to-pronounce, unfamiliar names and wondering why all these people were mentioned. We may even be tempted to skip ahead and continue with the next passage. But tucked into these genealogies are insights about God's faithfulness and goodness in our world.

The law of the Old Testament required the Israelites to keep genealogical records. In Numbers 3:10, God told Moses, "So you shall appoint Aaron and his sons, and they shall attend to their priesthood; but the outsider who comes near shall be put to death." To keep the law, the Israelites had to make sure anyone who served in the Levitical priesthood was a descendent of Aaron, of the tribe of Levi. The only way to assure this was to keep genealogical records.

No surprise genealogies appear throughout the Bible, but the only genealogies found in the New Testament appear in Matthew 1 and Luke 3.

Some genealogies cover a few generations while others cover centuries. Some genealogies tell exactly who parented whom, but others provide more broad strokes of lineage. Yet their inclusion in Scripture provides evidence of the historical authenticity of the Bible. They remind us that when we open the pages of Scripture we're reading of men and women who actually lived and were part of real families. Genealogies provide a chronology of events. Through them, we can help place events in subsequent order.

These records can also provide rich insights into Scripture. Studying the names of those listed can reveal clues to the people's personalities and character. Sometimes reading through a genealogy reveals an unexpected relationship between two people. Other times, genealogies reveal cultural backgrounds of different generations. And sometimes they show the connection between people who seem worlds apart.

Too often, we skim through biblical genealogies on to the next passage. With a fleeting glance, we skip the less engaging and impossible-to-pronounce names looking for more poignant stories. Yet, genealogies aren't something to be avoided but celebrated.

Genealogies remind us of God's loving commitment to humanity and His plan for redemption. Through these lists of names, we're reminded of both where we came from and where we're headed. And they remind us that the place in time God has us living is important. It's not an accident, but part of a greater story God is writing, in which we all play a role.

> Sometimes reading through a genealogy reveals an unexpected relationship between two people.

✤ Three Things to Remember

- Biblical genealogies are used as reminders that God is upholding the everlasting covenant with His people from generation to generation.

- Jewish culture did not require every name to be accounted for in a lineage to satisfy a genealogy.

- The main purpose of genealogies in Jewish culture was to establish familial roots or royal lineage.

1. How far back have you researched your genealogy? What do you know about your grandparents? Great-grandparents? Are you related to anyone noteworthy?

2. What are some benefits of knowing details about the lineage you came from?

Genealogy was important to many ancient cultures, including the Jewish people. The apostle Matthew begins his gospel with the genealogy of Jesus, marking the beginning of the arrival of the Messiah and the coming of the kingdom of God. Matthew uses this genealogy to trace the promises of God and show their fulfillment.

3. **Read Matthew 1:1–17**. Who does Matthew seem most concerned with linking Jesus to (hint: verse 17)? Why do you think Matthew wants to make this connection?

Matthew historically proves God has not forgotten His covenants with Israel, but is seeing them to fruition. He brings the King of the Jews, the Son of God, to reign and redeem the world. Yet some of the names listed in the genealogy are surprising.

4. Four scandalous women are listed in the lineage of Christ. According to the passages below, who are these women and what is scandalous about their stories?

Genesis 38:

Joshua 2:

Ruth 1:

2 Samuel 11:

5. Rather than hide these names, the gospel of Matthew declares them alongside Abraham, Isaac, and Jacob. Why would these specific women be mentioned at the beginning of Jesus' story? What does this reveal about God?

All four women mentioned were Gentiles. Tamar was an Aramean, Rahab was a Canaanite, Ruth was a Moabite, and Bathsheba was the wife of Uriah, a Hittite. Each of these women were considered outsiders to God's covenant because they weren't Jewish. Yet Matthew reminds us they were part of God's plan for salvation.

6. What do these women have in common with Mary, the mother of Jesus (hint: it has to do with Mary's pregnancy)?

7. Why would God choose to use prostitutes, Gentiles, and adulterers to bring about salvation?

8. What parts of your own heritage or story would you rather forget but God wants to use to bring salvation and healing to others?

Digging Deeper

The message of the Bible often seems upside down and paradoxical (e.g., a servant-king, to die is to live, the last shall be first, love your enemies). **Read 1 Corinthians 1:26–31.** We are all unworthy of Christ's sacrifice, so we can no longer boast in ourselves, but in Christ. Why do you think God chooses to use the lowly and despised? What does God's choice reveal about His love for you? For others?

✤ Personal Challenge

Instead of reading quickly through a genealogy like that found in Genesis 4:17–26 or Genesis 5, spend some time looking up the meanings of the names of those listed. You can do this simply by typing in the person's name along with "meaning of" into a search engine. Pay attention to how understanding the person's name adds meaning and understanding to the text.

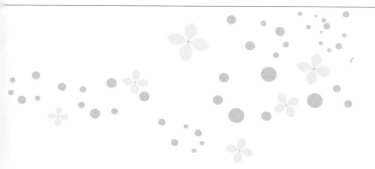

"Jesus of Nazareth could have chosen simply to express Himself in moral precepts; but like a great poet He chose the form of the parable, wonderful short stories that entertained and clothed the moral precept in an eternal form."

Dudley Nichols,
American screenwriter[1]

The Parables

The Power of Jesus' Stories

Jesus could have spent His time in ministry by providing direct teachings, but instead He surprised His listeners with challenging stories in the form of parables. By telling a story, Jesus taught people truths about God in an unexpected way that captured their imaginations, challenged their hearts, and called for a response.

Some of the parables Jesus taught were complete stories with a beginning, middle, and end. Others were more like comparisons to everyday life that made a great big God-concept more understandable.

In Matthew 13:44, Jesus compared the kingdom of God to a treasure hidden in a field. When a man discovered the field, he sold everything he had in order to buy it. Now a man didn't literally purchase a plot for buried treasure; the story is a parable meant to display what the kingdom of God is like with rich imagery and excitement.

Still other parables are metaphors or allegories. When Jesus revealed Himself as the "good shepherd" in John 10:11–16, He didn't actually pick up a staff and tell everyone to "baa" like sheep. Rather, He developed a poignant point of comparison as a means of revealing His identity and nature.

The parables of Jesus tend to be brief and concise. They were relatable to the everyday experiences of those who heard them. All of the parables center around God's kingdom. And many of them progress toward a conclusion we don't expect. For example, after reading of the bad behavior of the younger son in Luke 15, we don't expect the older son to also be hard-hearted.

Jesus' parables continue to confront us with profound truths, inviting us to become more Christlike and kingdom-oriented. Whenever we read one of Jesus' parables, we always need to consider the context—what happened just before and after the parable. Without the context, often the parable won't make much sense or we'll misinterpret it. At times, we need to compare the story with other stories to build our understanding and recognize what Jesus is calling us toward.

We also need to realize most of the time Jesus wanted to drive home a single point or idea in a parable. He wasn't using this form of storytelling to entertain people or display His cleverness, but to call people to respond to God. Therefore, when we read a parable, we, too, need to be ready to respond.

> All of the parables center around God's kingdom.

✤ Three Things to Remember:

- A parable is a story used to illustrate a spiritual truth.

- While studying parables, always read the surrounding text. What happens before and after each parable—the context—brings the story to life.

- Many times the characters in Jesus' parables stand for people He is speaking to. Be on the lookout for who represents whom in each story.

In Luke 8:10, Jesus states the purpose of a parable is to reveal truth to those who desire it and conceal truth from those who do not. Often, Jesus spoke in parables in the middle of conversations or in response to questions. Instead of giving direct answers, He told a story. Listeners drew their own conclusions.

1. **Read Luke 7:40–42**. What is the context—what's happening just before and after this parable?

2. What is the main idea or point of this parable?

The sinful woman shows her love for Jesus by washing His feet—a sign of respect and submission. Even more so, she washes His feet with expensive oil, tears, kisses, and hair. Unlike Jesus, the Pharisee doesn't have any compassion for this woman.

3. Who is representative of the creditor and the two debtors in this parable?

4. How do you think Simon identified with the parable as he heard it? How do you think the woman identified with the parable as she heard it?

In parables, Jesus not only addressed the issues of His time, but touched on issues we wrestle over even today. Jesus understood that a stumbling block for His followers would be how to manage wealth and resources. On one occasion, a man asked Jesus to take his side in an argument over money—much like a rabbi at the time would. Jesus reminds us through a parable there aren't any luggage racks on the hearse.

5. **Read Luke 12:16–21**. What is happening just before and after this parable? What is the main idea or point of this parable?

6. What warning does Jesus give to those who are more concerned about material possessions than spiritual things?

7. What is the right attitude toward material possessions in light of the kingdom of God?

8. What does it look like for you to be rich toward God in this season of your life?

Digging Deeper

Only two of the same parables appear in all three of the Synoptic Gospels (Matthew, Mark, and Luke): the parable of the soils and the parable of the wicked stewards. **Read the parable of the soils in Mark 4:1–20, Matthew 13:1–23, and Luke 8:4–18.** What are the common elements found in each of these parables? How do the parable accounts differ from each other? How would you describe the soil of your heart right now? What spiritual practices help you develop more fertile, rich soil?

✣ Personal Challenge

Sometimes the Bible can be challenging because it becomes too familiar. We know how a story will end, so we don't take time to slow down and allow each phrase and detail to sink in. Select a few parables and read them slowly. Imagine you're reading them for the very first time. Word. By. Word. Notice details. Savor the story. Invite God to speak to you through the Holy Spirit.

"Paul did not sit down one day and decide to write a textbook on doctrine. He wrote a *letter*."

Douglas J. Moo,
New Testament professor[1]

The Epistles
Love Letters to the Church

When was the last time you sat down and penned a handwritten letter to someone you cared about? Whom did you write to? What did you say?

The Epistles are like handwritten letters. They were written to specific people facing specific situations. The Epistles (*epistle* means "long, formal letter") refer to the twenty-one letters in the New Testament written by the apostles (people such as Peter, Paul, and Timothy) to either individuals or churches. They make up much of the New Testament. They include books like Romans, 1 and 2 Corinthians, Galatians, Ephesians, Philippians, Colossians, and many more.

Many of the Epistles follow a pattern. They often begin with a "to" and "from" revealing who wrote the letter and to whom the letter is addressed. Then there's often a warm greeting like "Grace to you and peace from God the Father and our Lord Jesus Christ" (Galatians 1:3), and a word of thanks or prayer. This is followed by the body of the letter, which closes with a final farewell such as

"Brethren, the grace of our Lord Jesus Christ *be* with your spirit. Amen" (Galatians 6:18).

These letters often challenged their readers to pursue God, avoid selfish and prideful attitudes, behave in a Christ-honoring way, live in unity, and adhere to the truths they'd learned from the apostles.

Some of the letters speak to false teachings circulating about Christ. Whenever reading an epistle, one must consider the cultural and historical situations these authors were addressing. Otherwise, understanding a passage or letter may be hard.

Take, for example, the letter to the Galatians. The Gentile churches in Galatia were impacted by teachers telling the believers they needed to obey Jewish customs in order to become Christians. In essence, they taught that salvation came through both obeying the entire Old Testament law and faith in Jesus. Paul wrote to the church of Galatia to expose this false teaching. He reminded the people of the good news extending to all and encouraged them to stand strong in the freedom given through Christ. Understanding what the Galatians were going through helps open up the Scripture and better understand it.

Reading the Epistles often reveals that the challenges the church faced thousands of years ago aren't much different now. These letters contain timeless truths that encourage and challenge us today.

These letters contain timeless truths that encourage and challenge us today.

✤ Three Things to Remember:

- The Epistles were written to instruct believers on living life as Christ-followers and as the body of Christ, His church.

- While reading the Epistles, note the circumstances and occasion for the writing. Many times this can be found in the opening salutation of the letter. If you're stumped, turn to a study Bible or commentary.

- Keep in mind the audience to whom each letter is written. Reading about the history of the early church in that particular city in a study Bible can help decipher meaning of certain passages.

The apostle Paul wrote to the people in Philippi, a Roman colony in the northern part of Greece known as Macedonia. Paul had planted a church there on his second missionary journey, and he wrote to them for a variety of reasons, including to thank and instruct his beloved friends. The Philippians had generously supported Paul in his ministry.

Philippians is the last of Paul's four epistles (including Ephesians, Colossians, and Philemon) written from a Roman prison. The Romans imprisoned Paul for his activities as a Christian.

1. **Read Philippians 1:1–11**. What does Paul's greeting and prayer reveal about his affection and hope for those living in Philippi? How does this warm salutation challenge you in the way you greet other believers?

Epistles were intended to be read aloud and in public, not just for the leader or pastor.

2. **Read Philippians 1:12–30**. Why is Paul concerned that those reading his letter know first about his circumstances? Why do you think this is important for Paul to communicate?

Paul rejoices with his friends in Philippi—no matter what the circumstance, Paul reminds them, they can be refined to be more like Christ. Philippians 2:6–11 contains a Christological hymn, probably used widely in the first-century church.

3. **Read Philippians 2:1–18**. What encouragement does Paul offer the Philippians in this passage? What about this passage is most encouraging for you in the situations you're currently facing?

4. **Read Philippians 2:19–30**. Who does Paul highlight in this passage? What does Paul communicate about these two people?

5. **Read Philippians 3**. What does Paul count as loss for Christ? What things have you counted as loss for Christ? How does this challenge you?

Paul's letters often have a section where they shift from theological to practical. Often, this is noted by the word *therefore*. Philippians 4 includes one of those shifts.

6. **Read Philippians 4**. Why should we learn to be content in our circumstances? How have you learned to be content in your circumstances?

7. Some of the most quoted scriptures are from this tiny book of Philippians. Reflecting on what you've read, which verses are most meaningful to you?

Paul encourages the Philippians to become more like Christ. This warm, friendly letter expresses thanks and contagious joy, despite Paul's imprisonment. Paul reminds us a life lived in pursuit of Christ brings abundant joy and happiness.

8. One of the ways we can nurture joy in our lives is by remembering all Christ has done for us. In the space below, make a list of ten things you're thankful for. Spend a few moments thanking God through prayer and worship for each one.

✤ ....

✤ ....

✤ ....

✤ ....

✤ ....

✤ ....

✤ ....

✤ ....

✤ ....

✤ ....

Digging Deeper

Nurturing joy and contentment is an ongoing process in our lives. **Read 1 Timothy 6:6–9 and 2 Corinthians 6:3–10**. How did Paul struggle to live joyfully and contentedly? How did Paul's choices and attitude enable him to overcome these struggles? What changes do you need to make in your choices and attitude to live with a greater joy and contentment?

✤ Personal Challenge

Pick up a commentary or Bible dictionary or spend some time online researching the city of Corinth and the people who lived there. Check out the location of Corinth on a map, the socioeconomic status of the people, and the culture of the region. Carve out time to read 1 or 2 Corinthians in a single sitting. Reflect on how understanding the political, economic, and social situation illuminates what Paul was saying to the church in Corinth.

"The true and living God summons us from our preoccupation with the world to recognize, in light of his ultimate plan for history, what really matters and what does not."

Craig S. Keener,
Biblical studies professor[1]

The Apocalyptic Literature
The Wondrous Mysteries of God

Have you ever traveled to a foreign country where you didn't know the language? A place where the signs were often impossible to comprehend? Where the customs seemed strange and even silly, and the ways of life were completely unfamiliar?

Sometimes that's what reading apocalyptic literature can feel like. With each passing page, we can feel like we're in a foreign land that's hard to understand and navigate. The imagery, symbolism, and mysterious declarations can leave us feeling bewildered or confused. But as we dig deeper, we can discover the writing's rich treasures.

Apocalyptic writing is a unique genre of writing in that it tells of future events without giving us all the details of what's going to happen. This type of literature is often marked by great hope, which encourages and challenges us to persevere through and overcome any persecution we face.

We find this type of writing appearing in books such as Isaiah, Daniel, and Ezekiel. It fills the pages of Zechariah and Revelation. Much of the writing has hidden meanings and symbolism presented in the forms of dreams and visions with sometimes bizarre imagery. That's why, when it comes to reading apocalyptic literature, it's a great idea to have a study Bible, commentary, and Bible dictionary in hand—along with a friend to discuss the passages along the way.

God will triumph.

While the prophets and Jesus used symbolic language, like salt and light, most of what they used was based on real things. In apocalyptic literature, we're introduced to wild images of things that don't exist—like a beast with seven heads and ten horns (Revelation 13:1) or locusts with scorpions' tails and human heads (Revelation 9:7–10). With such peculiar and downright weird symbolic language, it's easy to get distracted from the great truth that this writing conveys: no matter how bad the score might look mid-game, God wins in the end. Evil will be defeated. God will triumph.

One of the wonderful things about God hiding the details of the future from us is that it gives us the opportunity to seek God and depend on Him even more now. Another advantage is that in knowing God's long-term plans for the world, we're challenged to live faithfully no matter what we're facing today.

Apocalyptic literature grounds us in the truth of God's unrelenting love for us, His unending commitment to us, and the knowledge that in the end God and all those who choose to put their faith in Him will be victorious. Now that's reason to celebrate.

✤ Three Things to Remember:

- Much of the imagery described in apocalyptic literature has more than one interpretation or meaning. Consider reading articles or books from different perspectives to increase your understanding.

- When reading apocalyptic literature, stay alert to allusions or imagery found elsewhere in Scripture.

- Don't rely too heavily on the math. Numbers are used symbolically, not literally.

1. Have you ever traveled to another country or another part of your country where the culture, language, or way of life seemed foreign? If so, where did you go?

2. How did you learn to navigate through the foreign land?

Revelation is a book scholars will continue to wrestle over. Shrouded in mystery and overflowing with beauty, the apostle John's Revelation is a vision of what's to come. Part prophetic, epistle, and apocalyptic literature, Revelation describes a future utopia where God replaces the old creation with a new creation—the fulfillment of His promise to restore the world. Through the new heavens and new earth, God will reign over all and sin and death will be eradicated.

3. **Read Revelation 21:1–8**. What hope does the promise of verse 5, that God is making all things new, give you right now? What three things are you most ready for God to make new?

We're invited to the wedding to top all weddings—a celebration of the new heavens and new earth, marked by no more tears, sorrow, death, or pain, where God dwells among men. John describes a breathtaking city with gates open to people from all directions.

In ancient times, financial supporters had their names engraved on buildings they funded. In the same way, the names of God's people are etched into the gates and stones. From the streets to the walls, the entire city shouts of God's glory.

4. **Read Revelation 21:9–27**. Reflecting on this passage, what do you look forward to most in the New Jerusalem?

5. What things will not be in this new city (hint: verses 22–27)?

The final chapter in Scripture reveals the last testimonies of God revealed to John. God is the Alpha and the Omega, the beginning and the end. He is trustworthy and true to His covenantal promises with His people.

6. **Read Revelation 22**. What phrase is repeated three times in this chapter (hint: verses 7, 12, 20)? Why is this admonition so important? When are you most likely to forget or stop believing this powerful reminder?

7. What word is repeated multiple times in Revelation 22:17? How have you answered the invitation of this word in the past? How are you answering the invitation of this word today?

8. How does knowing God's plan for your future strengthen your faith for today?

Dig Deeper

A common theme in apocalyptic literature is throne imagery. In Revelation, John envisions the grandeur of God's throne. **Read Revelation 4**. What challenges you most about this scene from heaven? What is the response of those who dwell in the presence of God? Why is God worthy of your worship? What prevents you from worshiping God in the midst of your day to day?

✤ Personal Challenge

Sometimes we can be tempted to avoid reading apocalyptic literature because it's challenging. Commit to spending some time this week picking up a study Bible and reading through a few chapters in Revelation or the latter half of Daniel. Allow yourself to become more familiar with the text and comfortable with the mystery that surrounds this literature.

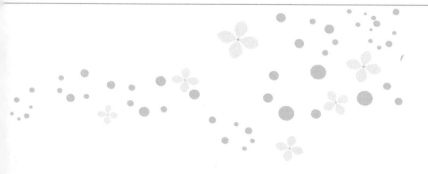

> "I encourage you to make the Bible part of your daily life. Don't worry about what you can't do; focus instead on what you can do—and then do it."

Billy Graham[1]

The Best Book Ever

Celebrating the Scripture Every Day

Sometimes referred to as the "Prince of Preachers," Charles Spurgeon was famed for preaching two services at his church in London to crowds of more than six thousand people. With more than twenty-five hundred of his sermons published, this famous preacher has more books in print than any other pastor in history.[2]

In one account from Spurgeon's life, a young pastor approached the famed preacher and asked if he'd listen to him teach and provide an assessment of the presentation. Spurgeon agreed. The young pastor preached a passionate sermon. He waited in expectation for Spurgeon's response.

Spurgeon observed that while the sermon was well-delivered and well-prepared, it was poor.

The young pastor pressed Spurgeon to know why.

"Because there was no Christ in it," Spurgeon replied.

"Well, Christ was not in the text, we are not to be preaching Christ always, we must preach what is in the text," the young pastor protested.

"Don't you know, young man, that from every town, and every village, and every little hamlet in England, wherever it may be, there is a road to London?"

"Yes," the young pastor answered.

"Ah!" Spurgeon said. "And so from every text in Scripture there is a road to the metropolis of the Scriptures, that is Christ. Dear Brother, when you get to a text, say, 'Now, what is the road to Christ?' and then preach a sermon, running along the road toward the great metropolis—Christ."[3]

God is waiting to meet you in the Bible!

Though every passage in the Bible is not explicitly about Christ, the Scriptures are constantly grounding us in the story of redemption and salvation that God has put in motion since the beginning of time, which finds its fulfillment in Jesus.

Our purpose in reading God's Word isn't to collect historical facts or to become a Bible trivia ninja, but to know and encounter God.

God is waiting to meet you in the Bible!

Sometimes as we read the Bible, we'll receive a word of encouragement and hope; sometimes we'll be faced with a word of confrontation. A passage may expose our pride or selfishness or personal idols and call us to repent that we can walk in greater holiness and freedom. But it's hard to read the Bible for very long and remain the same.

As we read, study, memorize, and savor Scripture, we can't help but grow in affection for God's Living Word—and more importantly, our love and appreciation for God and others will blossom too.

✛ Three Things to Remember:

- Christ redeeming and restoring the world was God's plan from the beginning.
- The gospel, the good news of Christ, is central to the Bible—from Genesis to Revelation.
- While knowing a lot about Bible stories or verses is valuable, the true importance is found in the transforming work God is doing in you as you read and study the Word.

1. When have you stumbled on a passage or verse that's been particularly meaningful to you? What impact have those words had on you?

Studying Scripture is something to be celebrated! God is constantly transforming us and revealing more of Himself through His Word. Whether we've read the same passage once or one hundred times, God continues to surprise us with His grace, mercy, and love, tucked into stories, verses, and passages.

2. **Read Psalm 19:7–14**. What words are used to describe God's Word in this passage? How have you found these to be true in your own life as you study Scripture?

The psalmist refers to God as the Redeemer in Psalm 19:14. *Redeemer* in the Old Testament means one who avenges, defends, vindicates, delivers, and rescues.

3. According to this passage, what do we gain by reading and studying God's Word?

At the beginning of His ministry, Jesus reveals the importance of knowing and understanding Scripture. Satan tempts Jesus to sin—even using Scripture out of context—but Jesus doesn't falter.

4. **Read Matthew 4:1–11**. What role did knowing Scripture play in Jesus' response to temptation? When has knowing a scripture helped you overcome temptation?

5. **Read John 8:31, 32**. What does Jesus say is one of the benefits of studying the Scripture? How have you experienced this in your own life?

After His death and resurrection, Jesus shrouds His identity and surprises a few of His friends.

6. **Read Luke 24:13–27**. What did Jesus choose to discuss with the men?

Even though Jesus spoke earlier of His suffering, death, and resurrection to His disciples, they still were afraid and unsure when He appeared to them.

7. **Read Luke 24:36–53**. How did Jesus choose to spend some of His final moments with the disciples (hint: verse 45)? What is one reason Jesus highlights that it's important to study the Old Testament (hint: verse 44)?

8. What prevents you from reading through the Old Testament more often? How does knowing that Christ is revealed in the Old Testament challenge you to dive into its pages?

Digging Deeper

Read John 14:23, 24. What does it look like for you to love God's Word? How do you show your affection for the Scripture on a daily basis? What changes can you make in your life to grow in your affection for the Bible and knowing God?

✤ Personal Challenge

If you've never read the entire Bible, would you consider reading through the Bible over the course of the next year? By committing to read three to four chapters a day, you'll cover Genesis to Revelation and have a better grasp on the great big story of God. Use a search engine online to find one-year Bible-reading plans. Take advantage of the opportunity to dive more deeply into the wonders of Scripture.

Leader's Guide

Chapter 1: The Bible
A Book Like No Other

1. The Bible may be an old or new friend, but reading Scripture is a discipline to be celebrated and enjoyed by every follower of Jesus.

2. Answers will vary. Encourage participants who struggle reading the Bible to pick up a more modern translation.

3. Answers will vary.

4. Paul lists issues from his time, such as people who are selfish, greedy, boastful, proud, blasphemers, unthankful, unholy, unloving, brutal, and more. Paul encourages Timothy to continue in the things he has learned and been assured of, including wisdom through Scripture and salvation through faith in Jesus.

5. Answers

Benefits of Scripture	How I've Experienced This in My Life
Doctrine	Answers will vary.
Reproof	
Correction	
Instruction	

6. Paul writes that Scripture prepares us to be equipped for every good work. We may have seen this to be true in difficult conversations with friends, in using Scripture for financial counsel, or in sharing the good news of Christ with others.

7. The Holy Spirit teaches and reminds us of the Word of God. Take a moment to ask the Holy Spirit to open up the Scriptures for each participant as you read the passages ahead. Celebrate what the Holy Spirit reveals and teaches in this time.

8. Many disciplines may be challenging at first, but when we continue to study and dive into God's Word, we will taste its sweetness. Spend time asking God to open each participant's eyes anew to Scripture.

Digging Deeper

As we read, study, and obey God's Word, our lives begin to reflect what we're learning. We become more grace-filled, more loving, and more merciful. Even when studying Scripture doesn't sound appealing, remember God is transforming us each time.

Chapter 2: The Law
A Portrait of the Character and Heart of God

1. God commanded the Israelites to leave the gleanings from the corners of their fields during harvest. By leaving this leftover crop, landowners allowed those less fortunate to harvest it for themselves and their families. This command reveals how intimately He cares for even the poor and the foreigner. Consider spending time at a local soup kitchen, offering to babysit for your neighbor's kids, or picking up extra groceries for the local food bank.

2. God commands that no one should steal, lie, swear, profane God's name, cheat, rob, harm the blind or deaf, be unjust, show partiality, hate, show vengeance, or hold a grudge. The Lord commands we love our neighbors

as ourselves. God deeply cares for each person and calls us to extend love and grace to those around us.

3. Answers will vary.

4.

Old Testament References	Commandment	New Testament References	How are they referenced?
Exodus 20:2, 3	No other gods	Matthew 4:10; 6:24	Then Jesus said to him, "Away with you, Satan! For it is written, 'You shall worship the LORD your God, and Him only you shall serve.'" "No one can serve two masters; for either he will hate the one and love the other, or else he will be loyal to the one and despise the other. You cannot serve God and mammon."
Exodus 20:4-6	No idolatry	1 John 5:21; 1 Corinthians 10:7	Little children, keep yourselves from idols. Amen. And do not become idolaters as *were* some of them. As it is written, "The people sat down to eat and drink, and rose up to play."
Exodus 20:7	Don't take the Lord's name in vain	Matthew 6:9; 1 Timothy 6:1	In this manner, therefore, pray: Our Father in heaven, hallowed be Your name. Let as many bondservants as are under the yoke count their own masters worthy of all honor, so that the name of God and *His* doctrine may not be blasphemed.
Exodus 20:8-11	Remember the Sabbath	Matthew 12:8; 12; Hebrews 4:9	For the Son of Man is Lord even of the Sabbath. Of how much more value then is a man than a sheep? Therefore it is lawful to do good on the Sabbath. There remains therefore a rest for the people of God.

Old Testament References	Commandment	New Testament References	How are they referenced?
Exodus 20:12	Honor your parents	Matthew 15:3, 4; 19:19; Ephesians 6:1–3	He answered and said to them, "Why do you also transgress the commandment of God because of your tradition? For God commanded, saying, 'Honor your father and your mother'; and, 'He who curses father or mother, let him be put to death.'" "'Honor your father and your mother,' and, 'You shall love your neighbor as yourself.'" Children, obey your parents in the Lord, for this is right. "Honor your father and mother," which is the first commandment with promise: "that it may be well with you and you may live long on the earth."
Exodus 20:13	Don't kill	Matthew 5:21, 22; Romans 13:9	"You have heard that it was said to those of old, 'You shall not murder, and whoever murders will be in danger of the judgment.' But I say to you that whoever is angry with his brother without a cause shall be in danger of the judgment. And whoever says to his brother, 'Raca!' shall be in danger of the council. But whoever says, 'You fool!' shall be in danger of hell fire." "For the commandments, 'You shall not commit adultery,' 'You shall not murder,' 'You shall not steal,' 'You shall not bear false witness,' 'You shall not covet,' and if there is any other commandment, are all summed up in this saying, namely, 'You shall love your neighbor as yourself.'"
Exodus 20:14	Don't commit adultery	Matthew 5:27, 28	"You have heard that it was said to those of old, 'You shall not commit adultery.' But I say to you that whoever looks at a woman to lust for her has already committed adultery with her in his heart."

Old Testament References	Commandment	New Testament References	How are they referenced?
Exodus 20:15	Don't steal	Matthew 19:18; Ephesians 4:28	"He said to Him, 'Which ones?' Jesus said, 'You shall not murder,' 'You shall not commit adultery,' 'You shall not steal,' 'You shall not bear false witness.'" "Let him who stole steal no longer, but rather let him labor, working with *his* hands what is good, that he may have something to give him who has need."
Exodus 20:16	Don't bear false witness	Matthew 12:36, 37; 19:18	"But I say to you that for every idle word men may speak, they will give account of it in the day of judgment. For by your words you will be justified, and by your words you will be condemned." "He said to Him, 'Which ones?' Jesus said, 'You shall not murder,' 'You shall not commit adultery,' 'You shall not steal,' 'You shall not bear false witness.'"
Exodus 20:17	Don't covet	Luke 12:15; 1 Timothy 6:10	And He said to them, "Take heed and beware of covetousness, for one's life does not consist in the abundance of the things he possesses." For the love of money is a root of all *kinds of* evil, for which some have strayed from the faith in their greediness, and pierced themselves through with many sorrows.

5. The focus of the first four commandments is honoring God.

6. The focus of the last six commandments is honoring others.

7. Commandments 1–4 challenge us to love God more. Commandments 5–10 challenge us to love others more. Answers will vary.

8. The law is the teacher which brings us to Jesus. The law establishes our need for grace. Almost no one can obey every one of God's commandments, which highlights our need for grace.

Digging Deeper

If the Israelites obey, God offers to give rain, plentiful harvests, full bellies, safety, strength in battle, fruitfulness, and His presence. If they disobey, God says He will allow terror, disease, bad harvests, defeat, oppression, and death. God blesses those who obey Him.

Chapter 3: Narrative History
Grasping the Big Story of God

1. Answers will vary. Encourage participants to spend time this week reading each person's story to familiarize themselves with each character.

2. Answers will vary. Invite participants to share a short example as to why they identified with certain characters.

3. Maybe David and Jonah encourage participants that God can still use us even when we've messed up. Perhaps Joseph's or Ruth's story assures us that God has a plan, even when we can't see the reasoning behind our circumstances.

4. If we only had read this part of David's stories, we would probably assume he was the bad guy or a bad king. We need to read the entirety of David's life in order to see why he was so near and dear to God's heart and how God redeems even the seemingly unredeemable.

5. This passage might conclude with what God thinks about the situation in order to contrast David's lack of interest in God's opinion. David continually tries to clean up his mess instead of asking God for forgiveness.

6. God's perspective is what is holy and pure. Our goal is to be transformed to be more like God. Therefore we must always look to what God thinks above what other people may think.

7. God's judgment is just. He will give retribution and right wrongs done to others. But God is still faithful. God does not leave David and listens to his cries of repentance. God even takes these cries into account when He passes judgment. God does not judge Solomon based on David's actions, but is faithful to David and loves his son.

8. Ultimately, God is the Hero of this narrative. He extends love toward David beyond what is expected.

Digging Deeper

Joseph's story reminds us that God has a plan for us even when He seems distant and we feel He doesn't care. Despite difficult circumstances, such as being sold into slavery or thrown in prison, we can rest assured that God is good always. No matter what circumstance we are facing, we know that God is in control.

Chapter 4: Wisdom Literature
Living the Best Possible Life

1. We may call on our best friend or spouse for advice on life's questions. Some of us may even turn to books or online resources to find wisdom in certain situations.

2. Encourage participants to briefly share a passage or story that assisted them in seeking wisdom and understanding.

3. Wisdom originates with the fear of the Lord. Proverbs enable us to have knowledge and to show justice, judgment, equity, and prudence.

4. This passage describes sinners enticing us to not walk in wisdom. The results of choosing this path is that they make haste to shed blood, lie in wait for their own blood, lurk secretly for their own lives, are greedy, and take away life.

5. For those who refuse to walk in wisdom, wisdom will laugh at their calamity, and mock when terror comes. The rewards of those who walk in wisdom is that they will dwell safely without fear of evil.

6. The rewards listed in this passage are long life, peace, favor in God's eyes, favor in man's eyes, paths directed by God, health, strength, full barns and vats, and God's delight.

7. To gain wisdom, we must ask God. He gives liberally and without reproach. Often, our stubbornness and pride may convince us we don't need wisdom or are wise enough.

8. Encourage participants to share at least one of their responses. Spend time praying together on these situations, and ask God for discernment and wisdom as we approach difficult decisions and circumstances.

Proverbs are highly practical because they deal with everyday occurrences. Proverbs don't support selfishness, and they encourage people to live wise lives.

Chapter 5: The Psalms
Timeless Songs and Prayers for Every Age

1. God displays His splendor in infants, animals, creation, man, the heavens, and more.

2. Children shout praise to Jesus, an affirmation of Psalm 8:2.

3. Answers

   Psalm 8:2: God has ordained strength out of the mouth of babes and nursing infants.

   Psalm 8:3, 4: God is mindful of man and visits him.

   Psalm 8:5–8: God made man a little lower than the angels, crowned him with glory and honor, and made him to have dominion over the work of God's hands.

   As the psalmist meditates on the splendors of God, he realizes the smallness of humanity compared to the vastness of God.

4. Our natural tendency may be to bring glory to ourselves. Psalm 8 challenges us to bring glory to God because He is so much greater and grander than us.

5. Psalm 3 contains an invocation for God (verse 1), a complaint of distress (verses 1, 2), a petition for intervention or vengeance (verse 7), a vow of

praise (verses 3, 4), an expression of trust in God (verses 5, 6), and a final praise (verse 8).

6. Perhaps a financial or relational struggle has challenged us to trust in God despite opposition.

7. Answers will vary. Encourage participants to read their laments out loud for the group, but be sensitive to anyone who doesn't feel comfortable. Begin by sharing yours.

8. When we bottle up our emotions from God, we build walls around our hearts. When we are honest with our emotions, even our fears and doubts, God offers freedom!

Digging Deeper

Both psalms describe God as King. The emotions expressed are those of praise and reverence. Allowing God to reign in our finances or in our relationships is often difficult. Ironically, when we allow God control in our lives, we can be set free from worry and stress.

Chapter 6: The Prophets
Calling People to Love God and Others

1. Riddle answer: A river. Riddles can confuse, irritate, or excite us. Use this question as an ice breaker to get to know the group a little better.

2. Answers will vary.

3. Answers will vary. Allow time for participants to be creative with this question—consider bringing in crayons, colored pencils, or markers.

4. God asks Ezekiel if the bones can live. Ezekiel responds that only God can know this. Ezekiel's answer to the question reveals he knows God is all-powerful and all-knowing. God knows what he does not. The question reveals God may have had something even bigger in mind than a mere answer. God has a much grander purpose planned.

5. Ezekiel did what the Lord commanded and the bones came to life. If Ezekiel hadn't responded in obedience, the bones may not have lived or God may have found someone else to do the job.

6. Life can leave us down for the count. We may experience times when we feel far from God or are unwilling to draw near to Him. In those times, God may use friends, spouses, teachers, books, sermons, movies, and more to breathe life back into us.

7. In Isaiah 61:1–3, the Spirit of the Lord is what enables the brokenhearted to be healed, the captives and prisoners set free into liberty, and a new way of living declared. In Matthew 3:16, the Holy Spirit descends on Jesus in the form of a dove before He launches His ministry on earth, declaring new life and freedom in Him. In Ezekiel 37:1–14, God's Spirit will be placed in those who have new life and liberty from the grave, and they will know God is the Lord.

8. Answers will vary. Spend time in prayer asking God to fill you with the strength, love, and mercy to breathe God's life into those people.

Digging Deeper

The Servant's humiliation will be overturned (52:13–15). The Servant will embody the power of God (53:1–3). The Servant will unnecessarily bear others' suffering (53:4–6). The Servant will be self-controlled (53:7–9). The Servant's suffering is God's will (53:1–12).

Chapter 7: The Gospels

Falling in Love with Jesus

1.

Passage	Fulfillment in Matthew
Isaiah 7:14	Therefore the Lord Himself will give you a sign: Behold, the virgin shall conceive and bear a Son, and shall call His name Immanuel.
Isaiah 60:3	The Gentiles shall come to your light, and kings to the brightness of your rising.
Isaiah 62:11	Indeed the LORD has proclaimed to the end of the world: "Say to the daughter of Zion, 'Surely your salvation is coming; behold, His reward *is* with Him, and His work before Him.'"
Micah 5:2	But you, Bethlehem Ephrathah, *though* you are little among the thousands of Judah, *yet* out of you shall come forth to Me the One to be Ruler in Israel, whose goings forth *are* from of old, from everlasting.

2. When we see how Jesus fulfilled prophecies, we can have further confidence He is the anticipated Messiah. Not only did God fulfill His promise of a Messiah, He continues to fulfill promises to us today.

3. In this passage, Jesus heals a woman in a crowd and raises Jairus's daughter from the dead. "Immediately" appears multiple times—depending on which translation you are reading from. (It occurs three times in the New King James Version.)

4. When we have faith, Jesus is quick to respond. The woman reaches for His cloak and is healed. Jairus has faith that Jesus can heal his daughter, and Jesus does so.

5. Spend time reading each of the stories found in Luke. Encourage participants to discuss what they think each one reveals about Christ's love and compassion.

6. Jesus loves without conditions—a tough goal to have. Ask God to open your eyes and heart to those on the margins and expand your capacity to love unconditionally.

7. John's purpose for writing is to prove that Jesus is the Son of God sent to redeem the world.

8. Consider setting aside time in the next few months to do a more in-depth study of that particular gospel.

Digging Deeper

Matthew begins with a genealogy, describing how Jesus is the long-awaited Messiah. Mark begins immediately with Jesus' launch into ministry. Luke sets up the birth of Christ. John begins with a cosmic poem. Depending on our personalities and what we enjoy reading, we may connect more with one gospel over another. However, when we read and study each one, we learn more about Christ from different perspectives.

Chapter 8: Genealogies
Hidden Treasures of the Bible

1. Use this question as an icebreaker for your time together. Spend time sharing what makes each person's family special and unique.

2. By studying our ancestry, we can learn how we're related to distant family members, our heritage, and how God has been faithful to our families over the years.

3. Matthew is making the link between Jesus and Abraham and David. The line of Abraham places Jesus in connection with the nation of Israel, and the line of David places Him in the royal lineage. Kings must have a royal lineage in order to be crowned. Matthew wants to validate that Jesus has the right to reign. The genealogy also connects Jesus with prophecies regarding the long-awaited Messiah.

4. **Genesis 38:** Tamar dressed as a prostitute to trick her father-in-law into sleeping with her and producing an heir.

   Joshua 2: Rahab was a prostitute and a traitor.

   Ruth 1: Ruth was a widow and a Moabite princess. The Moabites were enemies of the Israelites.

   2 Samuel 11: Bathsheba committed adultery with King David.

5. These women are listed to point out God can use anyone for His plan to redeem the world.

6. Mary is another unlikely character to be used by God, yet God uses her in an unforgettable way. As the other women in Jesus' genealogy have scandalous stories, Mary does too, as she became pregnant out of wedlock.

7. God is in the business of using imperfect, broken people to bring about His perfect will.

8. We may have rotten fruit on our family tree we want to forget. We may have shameful moments in our past we want to forget. However, Matthew 1 reminds us God can use anyone's story to bring about healing and salvation—even ours!

Digging Deeper

God has a heart for the broken and imperfect. He continues to use imperfect people as part of His master plan to save the world.

Chapter 9: The Parables
The Power of Jesus' Stories

1. Remind participants to read the context of the parable—what happens before and after. Before telling this parable, Jesus is confronted by a sinful woman who worships Him by anointing His feet. After the parable, Jesus connects His story with the woman whom Simon the Pharisee is judging.

2. Encourage participants to share their perspectives, which may differ. One of the main points of this parable is that those who need forgiveness the most and receive it will be the most grateful.

3. The creditor represents Jesus. The debtor who only owed fifty denarii represents the Pharisee. The debtor who owed five hundred denarii represents the sinful woman.

4. Simon probably felt the sting of rebuke as he realized how little hospitality and love he'd shown Jesus. The woman probably felt the acceptance and love of God as she heard the story.

5. Before Jesus tells the parable in Luke 12, a man asks Jesus to tell his brother to divide the inheritance. Directly after the parable is told, Jesus goes on to tell His disciples not to worry about anything because God cares for everyone. The main point of this parable is to not store up earthly treasures.

6. He warns them that God comes not for the treasures on earth, but for their souls.

7. In light of the kingdom of God, we should not worry about anything—our clothes, food, or shelter.

8. The parable Jesus tells in Luke 12 echoes truth into the modern day. We, too, wrestle with desiring and worrying about material possessions far more than our spiritual health.

Digging Deeper

In each gospel, Jesus tells the parable before a crowd, seeds are sown on four different types of ground, Jesus quotes from Isaiah, and then He explains the parable. Luke's account has a lot less detail, while Matthew's and Mark's expand on the setting, explanation, and grounds in which the seeds were sown. Encourage participants to share what soil their hearts reflect right now, but be sensitive by sharing yours first. Some spiritual practices include silence, making yourself quiet before God to hear His voice, and solitude—unplugging from the world and coming away for a time to be with Him.

Chapter 10: The Epistles
Love Letters to the Church

1. Paul's greeting reveals he deeply loves and cherishes the people of Philippi.

2. Paul wants readers to know about his circumstances first because he wants them to be bolder about speaking the Word and sharing about Christ. He reminds the church in Philippi that suffering for Christ is indeed something to be joyful about.

3. Paul encourages the Philippians to be united, to look out for the interests of others, to be humble as Christ is humble, and to do all things without complaining and disputing so that they may become blameless.

4. Paul highlights Timothy and Epaphroditus. Paul communicates Timothy's proven character as one who has served alongside Paul. Paul also communicates Epaphroditus's illness, which almost killed him. Because of Epaphroditus's work for Christ, he almost died.

5. Paul considers all things a loss for Christ. It can be tempting for us to put pride and worth in earthly things. Paul's message reminds us that Christ is worth far more than any earthly thing.

6. We should learn to be content in our circumstances and to rely on Christ's strength to do all things. God will supply our needs according to His riches in glory by Christ Jesus. In doing this, we become more like Christ. Encourage participants to share how they have learned to become more content.

7. Answers will vary.

8. Answers will vary.

Digging Deeper

In many of the situations Paul went through, such as imprisonment, long-term suffering, and sleeplessness, he could've easily struggled to live in joy and contentment. But Paul chose to act as a minister of God, to rejoice despite sorrow, and to live in love and godliness and patience. Encourage participants to share the changes they would like to make with a partner to be held accountable.

Chapter 11: The Apocalyptic Literature
The Wondrous Mysteries of God

1. Spend several minutes diving into this icebreaker question with the group.

2. For some, navigating through foreign lands can be stressful. Others may find joy in exploring the unfamiliar.

3. The idea that God makes all things new brings hope and joy. No matter what circumstances we may be going through or have gone through in the past, we can hold tight to God's promise.

4. Answers will vary.

5. There will be no temple, sun, moon, closed gates, night, or anything that defiles.

6. The repeated phrase is "Behold, I am coming quickly!" This admonition is an important reminder for us when we get caught up in the things of this world, rather than the things that God cares about—loving God and loving others.

7. The word *Come!* is repeated in Revelation 22:17. Answers will vary.

8. No matter what, God wins! We can have faith that in the end, everything is going to be okay.

Digging Deeper

Those who dwell in the presence of God respond in never-ending worship and adoration. Daily distractions like bills, carpools, deadlines, laundry, and more can keep us from worshiping God in the midst of our day-to-day.

Chapter 12: The Best Book Ever
Celebrating the Scripture Every Day

1. Encourage participants to share their favorite or life verses.

2. God's Word is perfect, sure, right, pure, true, righteous, more desirable than gold, and sweeter than honey.

3. According to this passage, we gain refreshment, wisdom, joy, light, reward, and blamelessness.

4. Jesus is able to recite passages from the Old Testament and refute what Satan says. Jesus correctly uses Scripture, whereas Satan twists and manipulates passages. When we have God's Word in our hearts, we can meditate on it and remember it even when we are pressed by temptation.

5. Jesus says one of the benefits of studying Scripture is freedom. Encourage participants to share how they have been set free by the truth found in Scripture.

6. Jesus hides His identity and tells the men that the story of Christ was told from Moses to the Prophets.

7. Jesus spends His final moments with the disciples explaining and opening their understanding of Scripture. It is important to study the Old Testament because Jesus fulfilled things written in the law of Moses, the Prophets, and the Psalms.

8. Often the Old Testament can seem distant and foreign from modern day. The stories and culture may be too hard to understand or be excited about. However, knowing that Christ is revealed in the Old Testament should excite and challenge us to dive headfirst into reading and understanding the Old Testament.

Digging Deeper

Loving God's Word may look like meditating, studying, or memorizing. Commit to reading passages from Scripture each day. Ask God to fill you with passion to know and understand God's Word.

Notes

Introduction

1. Charles Colson, *Loving God* (Grand Rapids: Zondervan, 1987), 55.

Chapter One

1. Frederick Buechner, *Wishful Thinking: A Seeker's ABC* (San Francisco: Harper San Francisco, 1973), 12.

2. H. A. Ironside, *In the Heavenlies* (New York: Loizeaux Brothers, 1949), 86–87.

Chapter Two

1. Ray Vander Laan, *God Heard Their Cry: Discovery Guide* (Zondervan: Grand Rapids, 2009), 15.

2. Gordon D. Fee and Douglas Stuart, *How to Read the Bible for All Its Worth: A Guide to Understanding the Bible* (Grand Rapids: Zondervan, 1981), 154–63.

Chapter Three

1. Gordon D. Fee and Douglas Stuart, *How to Read the Bible for All Its Worth: A Guide to Understanding the Bible* (Grand Rapids: Zondervan, 1993), 78.

Chapter Four

1. Paul E. Koptak, *The NIV Application Commentary* (Grand Rapids: Zondervan, 2003), 24–25.

Chapter Five

1. Ellen F. Davis, *Getting Involved With God: Rediscovering the Old Testament* (Cambridge: Crowley Publications, 1991), 5.

Chapter Six

1. Kenneth Scott Latourette, "Christianity Through the Ages," religion-online.org, http://www.religion-online.org/showchapter.asp?title=532&C=573.

Chapter Seven

1. John Calvin, *Golden Booklet of the True Christian Life*, trans. Henry J. V. Andel (Grand Rapids: Baker, 1952), 17.

Chapter Eight

1. Grant R. Osborne, *Exegetical Commentary on the New Testament: Matthew* (Zondervan: Grand Rapids, 2010), 68.

Chapter Nine

1. *Christianity Today Study Series: Faith and Pop Culture* (Nashville: Thomas Nelson, 2009), 35.

Chapter Ten

1. Douglas J. Moo, *The NIV Application Commentary: Romans* (Grand Rapids: Zondervan, 2000), 16.

Chapter Eleven

1. Craig S. Keener, *The NIV Application Commentary: Revelation* (Grand Rapids: Zondervan, 2000), 21.

Chapter Twelve

1. Billy Graham Evangelistic Association, "Spiritual Growth Topics," http://www .billygraham.org/spiritualgrowth_topics.asp?tid=31.

2. Rick Lawrence, *99 Thoughts on Jesus-Centered Living: Everyday Ways to Walk With the Rebel Jesus* (Loveland: Group Publishing, 2012), ii.

3. Sermon 242, *Christ Precious to Believers*, preached by Charles Spurgeon on March 13, 1859.

About the Author

Margaret Feinberg (www.margaretfeinberg.com) is a popular Bible teacher and speaker at churches and leading conferences such as Catalyst, Thrive, and Extraordinary Women. Her books and Bible studies have sold more than 600,000 copies and received critical acclaim and extensive national media coverage from CNN, the Associated Press, *USA Today*, *The Los Angeles Times*, *The Washington Post*, and more.

She was recently named one of the 50 Women shaping church and culture by *Christianity Today*, one of the 30 Voices who will help lead the church in the next decade by *Charisma* magazine, and one of the "40 Under 40" who will shape Christian publishing by *Christian Retailing* magazine. Margaret currently lives in Colorado with her husband, Leif, and their superpup, Hershey. One of her favorite treats is hearing from her readers, so connect with her on Facebook or Twitter @mafeinberg or drop her a note through her website.